ROCK
STEADY

A STORY OF NOAH'S ARK

ROCK STEADY

A STORY OF NOAH'S ARK

BY

STING

Illustrated by Hugh Whyte

HarperCollinsPublishers

About the Rainforest Foundation

The Rainforest Foundation US was founded from the demands of one man, and the vision of two people. The demand was made by Raoni, a chief of the Menkragnoti Kayapó who sought help to vocalize his people's plight and to protect their homelands in the heart of the Amazon Rainforest. Trudie Styler and Sting provided the vision; they took Raoni's story to the world and in doing so made millions of people aware of the looming ecological and cultural disaster that faced not only Raoni's people but the planet. From this initiative, the Rainforest Foundation US was born in 1989.

The Rainforest Foundation US
270 Lafayette Street, Suite 1107
New York, NY 10012
(212) 431-9098
http://www.savetherest.org

The Rainforest Foundation UK
http://www.rainforestfoundationuk.org

A Byron Preiss Book

Rock Steady
Lyrics and Musical Composition Copyright © 1987 by G. M. Sumner (p.k.a. Sting). All Rights Reserved.
Lyrics and Musical Composition administered by Magnetic Publishing Ltd./EMI Music Publishing Ltd.
Illustrations copyright © by Byron Preiss Visual Publications, Inc. and Hugh Whyte. Printed in the U.S.A. All rights reserved.
www.harperchildrens.com

Library of Congress Cataloging-in-Publication Data
Sting (Musician)
    Rock steady / Sting ; illustrations by Hugh Whyte.
        p.   cm.
    Summary: A verse retelling of Noah's Ark set in modern times.
    ISBN 0-06-029231-8 — ISBN 0-06-029232-6 (lib. bdg.)
    1. Noah's ark—Juvenile fiction.   [1. Noah's ark—Fiction.   2. Stories in rhyme.]   I. Whyte, Hugh, ill.   II. Title.
PZ8.3.S8585 Ro   2001
[E]—dc21
                                                                                                                                00-32036

1   2   3   4   5   6   7   8   9   10
❖
First Edition

For the benefit of the Rainforest Foundation

Saw an ad in the newspaper
That caught my eye.
I said to my baby, "This sounds
Like the ticket for you and I."

It said volunteers wanted
For a very special trip,
To commune with Mother Nature
On a big wooden ship.

We took a taxi to the river
In case any places were free.
There was an old guy with a beard,
And every kind of creature
As far as the eye could see.

This old guy was the boss.
He said, "I won't tell you no lie
But there's more to this journey
Than is apparent to the eye."

He said he'd heard God's message
On the radio.
It was going to rain forever
And He'd told him to go.

"I'll protect you all, don't worry,
I'll be a father to you all.
I'll save two of every animal,
No matter how small.

But I'll need some assistants
To look after the zoo.

I can't see nobody better,
So you'll just have to do."

I said, "Just tell me something
Before it's too late and we're gone.
I mean just how safe is this boat we'll be on?"

"It's Rock Steady, Rock Steady."

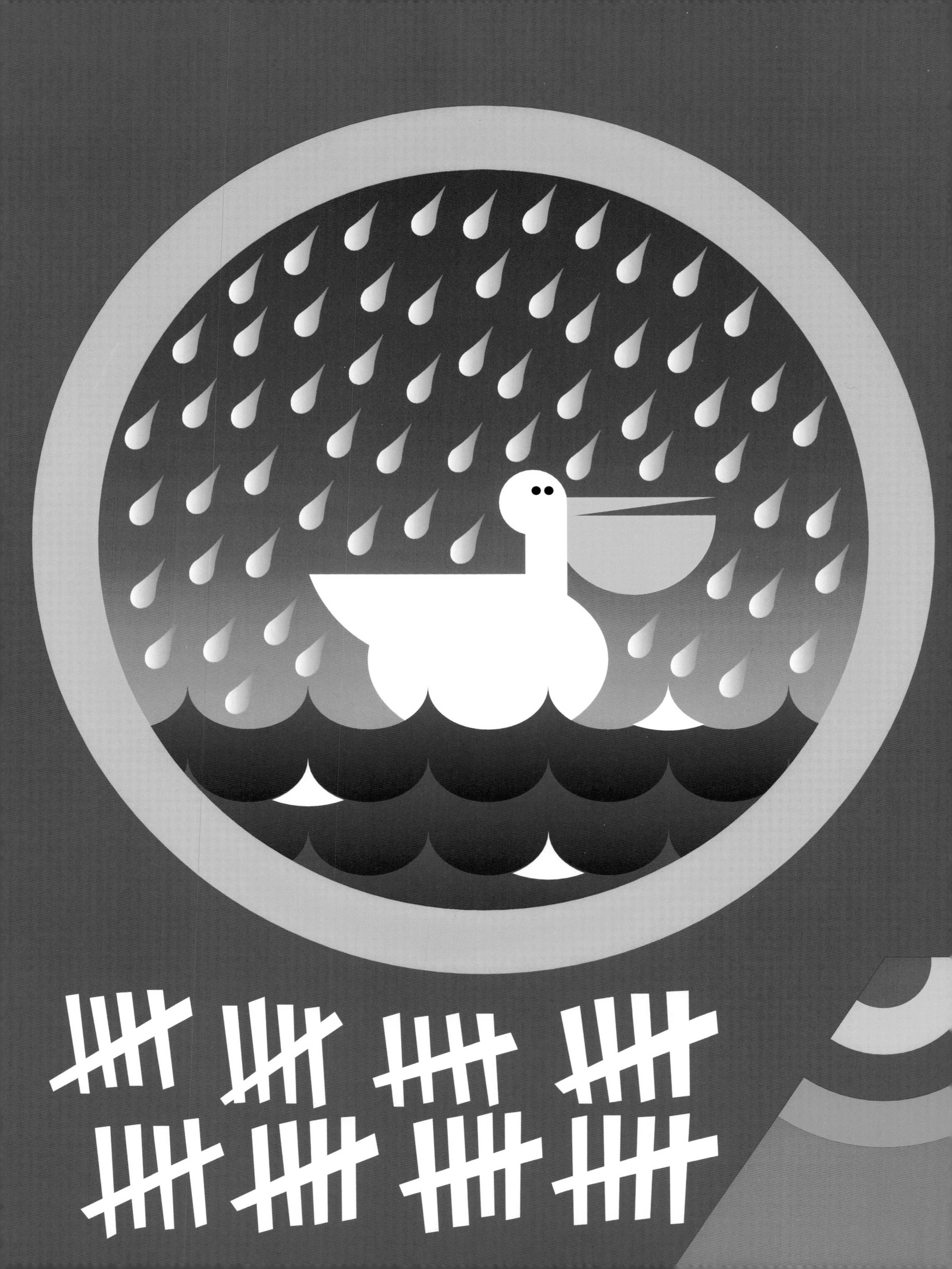

It rained for forty days
And forty long nights.
I'd never seen rain like it
And it looked like our old friend
Was being proved right.

We had no time to worry though.
There was too much to do.
We had to wash all the animals.
We had to feed them, too.

But we're as safe as houses,
As safe as mother's milk.
He's as cool as November
And as smooth as China silk.

He's God's best friend,
He's got a seat on the board,
And life may be tough,
But we're sailing with the Lord.

Rock Steady, Rock Steady.

Woke up this morning
And somethin' had changed,
Like a room in my house
Had just been rearranged.

She said, "It's stopped rainin'
And I know the guy's kind
But if we stay here much longer,
I'm gonna lose my mind."

So we said we had a mission
For his favorite dove,
To see if there was any mercy
From this great God above.

So to find dry land,
Away the white bird flew.
We didn't need no country.
Just a rock would do.

When the dove came back to us
He threw down a twig.

It was manna from heaven
And meant we would blow this gig.

"But the rock's too small," he said.
"Can't you see?" I said.
"It's just perfect for her.
It's perfect for me."

Rock Steady, Rock Steady.

Rock Steady, Rock Steady.

Rock Steady

Saw an ad in the newspaper that caught my eye.
I said to my baby, "This sounds like the ticket for you and I."
It said volunteers wanted for a very special trip,
To commune with Mother Nature on a big wooden ship.
We took a taxi to the river in case any places were free.
There was an old guy with a beard,
And every kind of creature as far as the eye could see.
This old guy was the boss. He said,
"I won't tell you no lie
But there's more to this journey than is apparent to the eye."
He said he'd heard God's message on the radio.
It was going to rain forever and He'd told him to go.
"I'll protect you all, don't worry.
I'll be a father to you all.
I'll save two of every animal, no matter how small.
But I'll need some assistants to look after the zoo.
I can't see nobody better, so you'll just have to do."
I said, "Just tell me something before it's too late and we're gone.
I mean just how safe is this boat we'll be on?"

"It's Rock Steady,   Rock Steady."

It rained for forty days and forty long nights.
I'd never seen rain like it and it looked like our old friend was being proved right.
We had no time to worry though. There was too much to do.
We had to wash all the animals. We had to feed them too.
But we're as safe as houses, as safe as mother's milk.
He's as cool as November and as smooth as China silk.
He's God's best friend, he's got a seat on the board,
And life may be tough, but we're sailing with the Lord.

Rock Steady,   Rock Steady.

Woke up this morning and somethin' had changed,
Like a room in my house had just been rearranged.
She said, "It's stopped rainin' and I know the guy's kind
But if we stay here much longer, I'm gonna lose my mind."
So we said we had a mission for his favorite dove,
To see if there was any mercy from this great God above.
So to find dry land away the white bird flew.
We didn't need no country, just a rock would do.
When the dove came back to us he threw down a twig.
It was manna from heaven and meant we would blow this gig
"But the rock's too small," he said.
"Can't you see?" I said.
"It's just perfect for her. It's perfect for me."

Rock Steady,   Rock Steady.